THE
PYTHON BIBLE

VOLUME ONE

INTRODUCTION AND BASICS

BY

FLORIAN DEDOV

TABLE OF CONTENT

INTRODUCTION

This book is the first part of a series that is called the Python Bible. In this series, we are going to focus on learning the Python programming language as effective as possible. The goal is to learn it smart and fast without needing to read thousands of pages. We will keep it simple and precise.

In this first book, we will introduce you to the language and learn the basics. It is for complete beginners and no programming, IT or math skills are needed to understand it. At the end, you will be able to write some simple and interesting programs and you will have the necessary basis to continue with volume two.

WHY PYTHON?

One question you might be asking yourself right now is: Why learn Python? Why not Java, C++ or Go?

First of all, a good programmer is fluent in multiple languages, so learning Python doesn't mean that you can't learn C++ or Java additionally. But second of all, Python is probably the best language to start with.

It is extremely simple in its syntax (the way the code is written) and very easy to learn. A lot of things that you need to do manually in other languages are automated in Python.

Besides that, Python's popularity is skyrocketing. According to the TIOBE-Index, Python is the third most popular language with an upward trend. But also in other rankings, you will see Python near the top.

TIOBE: https://www.tiobe.com/tiobe-index/

Also, Python is the lingua franca of machine learning. This means that it is the one language that is used the most in the areas of artificial intelligence, data science, finance etc. All these topics will be part of this Python Bible series. But since Python is a general-purpose language, the fields of application are numerous.

Last but not least, Python is a very good choice because of its community. Whenever you have some problem or some error in your code, you can go online and find a solution. The community is huge and everything was probably already solved by someone else.

HOW TO READ THIS BOOK

In order to get as much value as possible from this book, it is very important that you code the individual examples yourself. When you read and understand a new concept, play around with it. Write some scripts and experiment around. That's how you learn and grow.

So, stay motivated. Get excited and enjoy your programing journey. If you follow the steps in this book, you will have a solid basis and a decent understanding of the Python language. I wish you a lot of fun and success with your code!

Just one little thing before we start. This book was written for you, so that you can get as much value as possible and learn to code effectively. If you find this book valuable or you think you learned something new, please write a quick review on Amazon. It is completely free and takes about one minute. But it helps me produce more high quality books, which you can benefit from.

Thank you!

If you are interested in free educational content about programming and machine learning, check out: https://www.neuralnine.com/

1 – INSTALLING PYTHON

Now, before we get into the code, we need to install Python and our development environment. Python is a so-called *interpreted* language. This means that the code needs a certain software (the interpreter) to be executed.

Other languages like C++ or Java are *compiled* languages. You need a compiler but then the program is converted into machine code and can be executed without extra software. Python scripts can't be executed without a Python interpreter.

PYTHON INSTALLATION

First of all, you need to visit the official Python website in order to get the latest version from there.

Python: https://www.python.org/downloads/

Download the installer and follow the instructions. Once you are done, you should have the Python interpreter as well as the IDLE on your computer.

The IDLE is an *Integrated Development and Learning Environment*. It is the basic editor, where we can write and execute our code. Just open your start menu and look for it.

DEVELOPMENT ENVIRONMENT

PYTHON IDLE

When it comes to our development environment, we have many options to choose from. The simplest choice is to just use the default IDLE. It is a great tool for writing the code and it has an integrated interpreter. So, you can execute the code directly in the IDLE. For beginners this is definitely enough. If you choose this option, you can just stick with the basic installation. In this book, we are going to assume that you are using the IDLE.

EDITOR AND CLI

If you prefer to use a specific editor, like Atom, Sublime or VS Code, you can run your code directly from the command line. So you basically write your code in your editor and save the file. Then you run CMD (on Windows) or Terminal (on Linux & Mac). You need to use the following syntax in order to run the code:

```
python <scriptname>.py
```

This option is a bit less convenient but if you prefer using a specific editor, you may need to do it. Another way would be to look for some Python interpreter plugins for your editor.

Atom Editor: https://atom.io/

Sublime Text: https://www.sublimetext.com/

VS Code: https://code.visualstudio.com/

PYCHARM

Last but not least, you can also decide to use a very professional IDE with a lot of features. For Python this is PyCharm. This development environment is a product of JetBrains, a very well-known and professional company. It has a ton of features, professional syntax highlighting and a great user interface. I would definitely recommend it to every Python developer, but I think it might be a bit too much and not necessary for beginners. But that is your decision. If you are interested, you can get the community edition for free.

PyCharm: https://www.jetbrains.com/pycharm/

Now, let's get into the code!

2 – OUR FIRST PROGRAM

In order to understand the syntax of Python, we are going to start with a very simple first program. It is a tradition in programming to start with a *Hello World* application, when you are learning a new language. So, we are going to do that in this chapter.

HELLO WORLD

A *Hello World* application is just a script that outputs the text *"Hello World!"* onto the screen. In Python this is especially simple.

```python
print("Hello World!")
```

As you can see, this is a one-liner in Python. In other languages, we would have to define a basic structure with functions, classes and more, just to print one text.

But let's see what's happening here. The first thing that we can notice is the so-called *function* with the name *print*. When we use that function, it outputs a certain text onto the screen. The text that we want to print needs to be put between the parentheses.

Another thing that is very important here, are the quotation marks. They indicate that the text is a *string* and not a name of something else. A string is a data-type that represents text. When we don't use quotation marks, the interpreter will think that *Hello World!* is a variable name and not a text. Therefore, we will get an error message. But we will talk about variables and data types in the next chapter.

RUNNING THE SCRIPT

Now, we just need to run the script we just wrote. For that, you need to save the script into a Python file. Then you can use the integrated interpreter of the IDLE. Just click on Run -> Run Module (or F5).

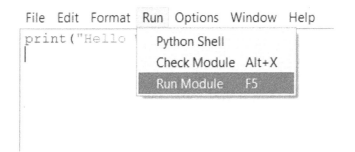

Running Code in Python IDLE

You will then see the results on the screen. That's how you run your first program.

3 – VARIABLES AND DATA TYPES

Probably, you have already encountered variables in your math classes. Basically, they are just placeholders for values. In programming, that's the same. The difference is that we have a lot of different data types, and variables cannot only store values of numbers but even of whole objects.

In this chapter we are going to take a look at variables in Python and the differences of the individual data types. Also, we will talk about type conversions.

NUMERICAL DATA TYPES

The types you probably already know from mathematics are numerical data types. There are different kinds of numbers that can be used for mathematical operations.

NUMERICAL DATA TYPES		
DATA TYPE	KEYWORD	DESCRIPTION
Integer	int	A whole number
Float	float	A floating point number
Complex	complex	A complex number

As you can see, it's quite simple. An integer is just a regular whole number, which we can do basic calculations with. A float extends the integer and allows decimal places because it is a floating point number. And a complex number is what just a number that has a *real* and an *imaginary* component. If you don't understand complex numbers mathematically, forget about them. You don't need them for your programming right now.

STRINGS

A string is just a basic sequence of characters or basically a text. Our text that we printed in the last chapter was a string. Strings always need to be surrounded by quotation marks. Otherwise the interpreter will not realize that they are meant to be treated like text. The keyword for String in Python is *str*.

BOOLEANS

Booleans are probably the most simple data type in Python. They can only have one of two values, namely *True* or *False*. It's a binary data type. We will use it a lot when we get to conditions and loops. The keyword here is *bool*.

SEQUENCES

Sequences are a topic that we will cover in a later chapter. But since sequences are also data types we will at least mention that they exist.

SEQUENCE TYPES		
DATA TYPE	**KEYWORD**	**DESCRIPTION**
List	list	Collection of values
Tuple	tuple	Immutable list
Dictionary	dict	List of key-value pairs

CREATING VARIABLES

Creating variables in Python is very simple. We just choose a name and assign a value.

```
myNumber = 10
myText = "Hello"
```

Here, we defined two variables. The first one is an integer and the second one a string. You can basically choose whatever name you want but there are some limitations. For example you are not allowed to use reserved keywords like *int* or *dict*. Also, the name is not allowed to start with a number or a special character other than the underline.

USING VARIABLES

Now that we have defined our variables, we can start to use them. For example, we could print the values.

```
print(myNumber)
print(myText)
```

Since we are not using quotation marks, the text in the parentheses is treated like a variable name.

Therefore, the interpreter prints out the values *10* and *"Hello"*.

TYPECASTING

Sometimes, we will get a value in a data type that we can't work with properly. For example we might get a string as an input but that string contains a number as its value. In this case *"10"* is not the same as *10*. We can't do calculations with a string, even if the text represents a number. For that reason we need to typecast.

```
value = "10"
number = int(value)
```

Typecasting is done by using the specific data type function. In this case we are converting a string to an integer by using the *int* keyword. You can also reverse this by using the *str* keyword. This is a very important thing and we will need it quite often.

4 – OPERATORS

The next thing we are going to learn is operators. We use operators in order to manage variables or values and perform operations on them. There are many different types of operators and in this chapter we are going to talk about the differences and applications.

ARITHMETIC OPERATORS

The simplest operators are arithmetic operators. You probably already know them from mathematics.

ARITHMETIC OPERATORS		
OPERATOR	**NAME**	**DESCRIPTION**
+	Addition	Adds two values
-	Subtraction	Subtracts one value from another
*	Multiplication	Multiplies two values
/	Division	Divides one value by another
%	Modulus	Returns the remainder of a division
**	Exponent	Takes a value to the power of another value
//	Floor Division	Returns the result of a division without decimal places

Let's take a look at some examples.

20 + 10 = 30   20 - 10 = 10

2 * 10 = 20   5 / 2 = 2.5

5 % 2 = 1   5 ** 2 = 25

5 // 2 = 2

If you don't get it right away, don't worry. Just play around with the operators and print the results. Of course you can also use variables and not only pure values.

ASSIGNMENT OPERATORS

Another type of operators we already know is assignment operators. As the name already tells us, we use them to assign values to variables.

ASSIGNMENT OPERATORS	
OPERATOR	**DESCRIPTION**
=	Assigns a value to a variable
+=	Adds a value to a variable
-=	Subtracts a value from a variable
*=	Multiplies a value with a variable
/=	Divides the variable by a value
%=	Assigns the remainder of a division
**=	Assigns the result of a exponentiation
//=	Assigns the result of a floor division

Basically we use these operators to directly assign a value. The two statements down below have the same effect. It's just a simpler way to write it.

```
a = a + 10
a += 10
```

COMPARISON OPERATORS

When we use comparison operators in order to compare two objects, we always get a Boolean. So our result is binary, either True or False.

COMPARISON OPERATORS		
OPERATOR	**NAME**	**DESCRIPTION**
==	Equal	Two values are the same
!=	Not Equal	Two values are not the same
>	Greater Than	One value is greater than the other
<	Less Than	One value is less than the other
>=	Greater or Equal	One value is greater than or equal to another
<=	Less or Equal	One value is less than or equal to another

We use comparisons, when we are dealing with conditions and loops. These are two topics that we will cover in later chapters.

When a comparison is right, it returns True, otherwise it returns False. Let's look at some examples.

10 == 10 → **True**   10 != 10 → **False**

20 > 10 → **True**   20 > 20 → **False**

20 >= 20 → **True**   20 < 10 → **False**

10 <= 5 → **False**

LOGICAL OPERATORS

Logical operators are used to combine or connect Booleans or comparisons.

LOGICAL OPERATORS	
OPERATOR	**DESCRIPTION**
or	At least one has to be *True*
and	Both have to be *True*
not	Negates the input

I think this is best explained by examples, so let's look at some.

True or **True** → **True**   **True** and **True** → **True**

True or **False** → **True**   **False** and **False** → **False**

False or **False** → **False**   not **True** → **False**

True and **False** → **False**   not **False** → **True**

OTHER OPERATORS

There are also other operators like bitwise or membership operators. But some of them we just don't need and others need a bit more programming knowledge to be understood. So for this chapter we will stick with those.

5 – USER INPUT

Up until now, the only thing we did is to print out text onto the screen. But what we can also do is to input our own data into the script. In this chapter, we are going to take a look at user input and how to handle it.

INPUT FUNCTION

In Python we have the function *input*, which allows us to get the user input from the console application.

```
name = input("Please enter your name:")
print(name)
```

Here, the user can input his name and it gets saved into the variable *name*. We can then call this variable and print it.

```
number1 = input("Enter first number: ")
number2 = input("Enter second number: ")
sum = number1 + number2
print("Result: ", sum)
```

This example is a bit misleading. It seems like we are taking two numbers as an input and printing the sum. The problem is that the function *input* always returns a string. So when you enter 10, the value of the variable is *"10"*, it's a string.

So, what happens when we add two strings? We just append one to the other. This means that the sum of

"15" and "26" would be "1526". If we want a mathematical addition, we need to typecast our variables first.

```
number1 = input("Enter first number: ")
number2 = input("Enter second number: ")
number1 = int(number1)
number2 = int(number2)
sum = number1 + number2
print("Result: ", sum)
```

Now our script works well! Always remember that the input function returns a string and you need to typecast it, if you want to do calculations with it.

6 – CONDITIONS

This chapter is about a concept that will make our scripts more interesting. So far, the interpreter always executed one command after the other. With conditions, this changes.

IF, ELIF, ELSE

Basically, a condition needs to return *True*, so that our script continues with the code in its block.

```
number = input("Enter a number:")
number = int(number)

if number < 10:
    print("Your number is less than 10")
elif number > 10:
    print("Your number is greater than 10")
else:
    print("Your number is 10")
```

The three important keywords here are *if, elif* and *else*. In this script, the user inputs a number that gets converted into an integer. Then our first *if-statement* checks if this number is less than ten. Remember that comparisons always return *True* or *False*. If the return is *True*, the code that is indented here gets executed. We use colons and indentations to mark code blocks in Python.

If this condition returns *False*, it continues to the *elif-block* and checks if this condition is met. The same procedure happens here. You can have as many *elif-blocks* as you want. If no condition is met, we get into the *else-block*.

FLOWCHART

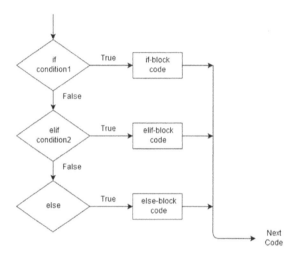

In this flowchart you can see how these basic if, elif and else trees work. Of course, you don't need an elif or else block. You can just write an if-statement and if the condition is not met, it skips the code and continues with the rest of the script.

NESTED IF-STATEMENTS

You can also put if-blocks into if-blocks. These are called *nested* if-statements.

```
if number % 2 == 0:
    if number == 0:
        print("Your number is even but
zero")
    else:
        print("Your number is even")
else:
    print("Your number is odd")
```

So, here we have the first condition, which checks if the number is even. When it's even it then checks if it's a zero or not. That's a trivial example but you get the concept.

7 – LOOPS

If we want to automate a repetitive process, we can use loops to do that. A loop is a programming structure that executes the same code over and over again, as long as a certain condition is met. This is at least true for the classic *while loop.*

WHILE LOOP

There are two types of loops in Python: *while loops* and *for loops*. A while loop executes the code in its block *while* a condition is met.

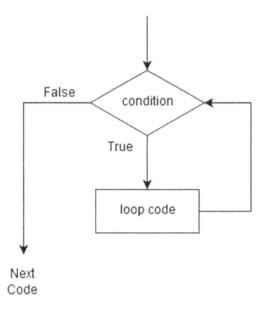

As you can see, it goes in circles until the condition returns *False*. Let's have a look at the code.

```
number = 0
while number < 10:
    number += 1
    print(number)
```

We use the *while* keyword to define the loop. Then we state a condition and again the code block is indented after the colon. In this example, we are counting from one to ten. We are initializing the variable *number* with the value zero. In every iteration, we increase it by one and print its value. This is done as long as the number is less than ten.

ENDLESS LOOP

With this knowledge, we can create an endless loop. This might seem useless but in fact it has some applications.

```
while True:
    print("This will print forever")
```

It is done by defining a loop which has the condition *True*. Since it is always *True*, the loop will never end, unless we terminate the script.

Warning: This might overload your computer, especially if it is a slow one.

FOR LOOP

The *for loop* works a bit differently. Here we don't have a condition. This loop type is used to iterate over sequences. Since these are the topic of the next chapter, we won't get into too much detail here.

```
numbers = [10, 20, 30, 40]
for number in numbers:
    print(number)
```

For now, we won't care about the syntax of sequences. Just notice that we have a list of four numbers. We then use the *for* keyword to iterate over it. The control variable *number* always gets assigned the value of the next element. In this case, we print out all the numbers.

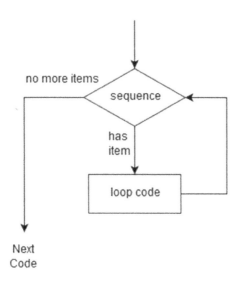

As you can see, the loop continues as long as there is a next element in the list.

RANGE FUNCTION

With the *range* function, we can create lists that contain all numbers in between two numbers.

```
for x in range(100):
    print(x)
```

This right here is a simple way to print all the numbers up to 100. But what you can also do is start counting from another number.

```
for x in range (20, 80):
    print(x)
```

Our range list here contains the numbers between 20 and 80.

LOOP CONTROL STATEMENTS

In order to manage loops, we have so-called *loop control statements*. They allow us to manipulate the process flow of the loop at a specific point.

BREAK STATEMENT

With the *break* statement, we can end a loop immediately, without caring about the condition.

```
number = 0
while number < 10:
    number += 1
    if number == 5:
        break
    print(number)
```

Here, we have a simple counting loop. As soon as the number reaches the value five, we execute a break statement and the script continues with the rest of the code.

CONTINUE STATEMENT

If we don't want to break the full loop, but to skip only one iteration, we can use the *continue* statement.

```
number = 0
while number < 10:
    number += 1
    if number == 5:
        continue
    print(number)
```

In this example, we always increase the number by one and then print it. But if the number is a five, we skip the iteration, after the increment. So, this number doesn't get printed.

PASS STATEMENT

The *pass* statement is a very special statement, since it does absolutely nothing. Actually, it is not really a loop control statement, but a placeholder for code.

```python
if number == 10:
    pass
else:
    pass

while number < 10:
    pass
```

Sometimes you want to write your basic code structure, without implementing the logic yet. In this case, we can use the pass statement, in order to fill the code blocks. Otherwise, we can't run the script.

8 – SEQUENCES

The sequence is the most basic data structure in Python. It contains multiple elements and they are indexed with a specific number. In this chapter, we are going to talk about the different types of sequences and their functions.

LISTS

The first sequence type we are looking at is the list. It is what the name says – just a list.

```python
numbers = [10, 22, 6, 1, 29]
```

In Python, we define lists by using square brackets. We put the elements in between of those and separate them by commas. The elements of a list can have any data type and we can also mix them.

```python
numbers = [10, 22, 6, 1, 29]
names = ["John", "Alex", "Bob"]
mixed = ["Anna", 20, 28.12, True]
```

ACCESSING VALUES

In order to access values of a sequence, we need to first talk about indices. The index is more or less the position of the element. What's important here is that we start counting from zero. So the first element has the index zero, the second has the index one and so on. We can then access the element by using the index.

```
print(numbers[2])
print(mixed[1])
print(names[0])
```

We print the third element of *numbers* (6), the second element of *names* (Alex) and the first element of *mixed* (Anna).

But instead of only accessing one single element, we can also define a range that we want to access.

```
print(numbers[1:3])   # 22 and 6
print(numbers[:3])    # 10, 22 and 6
print(numbers[1:])    # 22, 6, 1 and 29
```

By using the colon, we can slice our lists and access multiple elements at once.

MODIFYING ELEMENTS

In a list, we can also modify the values. For this, we index the elements in the same way.

```
numbers[1] = 10
names[2] = "Jack"
```

The second element of the numbers list is now *10* instead of *22* and the third element of the names list is *Jack* instead of *Bob*.

LIST OPERATIONS

Some of the operators we already know can be used when working with lists – addition and multiplication.

LIST OPERATIONS	
OPERATION	**RESULT**
[10, 20, 30] + [40, 50, 60]	[10, 20, 30, 40, 50, 60]
[10, "Bob"] * 3	[10, "Bob", 10, "Bob", 10, "Bob"]

LIST FUNCTIONS

When it comes to lists, there are a lot of different functions and methods that we can use. We are not going to talk about all of them, since it's just not necessary. Our focus will lie on the most important ones.

LIST FUNCTIONS	
FUNCTION	**DESCRIPTION**
len(list)	Returns the length of a list
max(list)	Returns the item with maximum value
min(list)	Returns the item with minimum value
list(element)	Typecasts element into list

LIST METHODS	
METHOD	**DESCRIPTION**
list.append(x)	Appends element to the list

list.count(x)	Counts how many times an element appears in the list
list.index(x)	Returns the first index at which the given element occurs
list.pop()	Removes and returns last element
list.reverse()	Reverses the order of the elements
list.sort()	Sorts the elements of a list

TUPLES

The next sequence type we are going to look at is very similar to the list. It's the *tuple*. The only difference between a list and a tuple is that a tuple is immutable. We can't manipulate it.

```
tpl = (10, 20, 30)
```

Notice that a tuple is defined by using parentheses rather than square brackets.

TUPLE FUNCTIONS

Basically, all the reading and accessing functions like *len, min* and *max* stay the same and can be used with tuples. But of course it is not possible to use any modifying or appending functions.

DICTIONARIES

The last sequence type in this chapter will be the *dictionary*. A dictionary works a bit like a lexicon. One element in this data structure points to another. We are talking about key-value pairs. Every entry in this sequence has a key and a respective value. In other programming languages this structure is called *hash map*.

```
dct = {"Name": "John",
       "Age": 25,
       "Height": 6.1}
```

We define dictionaries by using curly brackets and the key-value pairs are separated by commas. The key and the value themselves are separated by colons. On the left side there is the key and on the right side the according value.

Since the key now replaces the index, it has to be unique. This is not the case for the values. We can have many keys with the same value but when we address a certain key, it has to be the only one with that particular name. Also keys can't be changed.

ACCESSING VALUES

In order to access values of a dictionary, we need to address the keys.

```
print(dct["Name"])
print(dct["Age"])
print(dct["Height"])
```

Notice that if there were multiple keys with the same name, we couldn't get a result because we wouldn't know which value we are talking about.

DICTIONARY FUNCTIONS

Similar to lists, dictionaries also have a lot of functions and methods. But since they work a bit differently and they don't have indices, their functions are not the same.

DICTIONARY FUNCTIONS	
FUNCTION	**DESCRIPTION**
len(dict)	Returns the length of a dictionary
str(dict)	Returns the dictionary displayed as a string

DICTIONARY METHODS	
METHOD	**DESCRIPTION**
dict.clear()	Removes all elements from a dictionary
dict.copy()	Returns a copy of the dictionary
dict.fromkeys()	Returns a new dictionary with the same keys but empty values
dict.get(key)	Returns the value of the given key

dict.has_key(key)	Returns if the dictionary has a certain key or not
dict.items()	Returns all the items in a list of tuples
dict.keys()	Returns a list of all the keys
dict.update(dict2)	Add the content of another dictionary to an existing one
dict.values()	Returns a list of all the values

MEMBERSHIP OPERATORS

One type of operators we haven't talked about yet is membership operators. These are very important when it comes to sequences. We use them to check if an element is a member of a sequence, but also to iterate over sequences.

```
list1 = [10, 20, 30, 40, 50]
print(20 in list1)      # True
print(60 in list1)      # False
print(60 not in list1)  # True
```

With the *in* or *not in* operators, we check if a sequence contains a certain element. If the element is in the list, it returns *True*. Otherwise it returns *False*.

But we also use membership operators, when we iterate over sequences with for loops.

```
for x in list1:
    print(x)
```

For every element *in* the sequence *x* becomes the value of the next element and gets printed. We already talked about that in the loops chapter.

9 – FUNCTIONS

Oftentimes in programming, we implement code that we want to use over and over again at different places. That code might become quite large. Instead of re-writing it everywhere we need it, we can use *functions*.

Functions can be seen as blocks of organized code that we reuse at different places in our scripts. They make our code more modular and increase the reusability.

DEFINING FUNCTIONS

In order to define a function in Python, we use the *def* keyword, followed by a function name and parentheses. The code needs to be indented after the colon.

```
def hello():
    print("Hello")
```

Here we have a function *hello* that prints the text *"Hello"*. It's quite simple. Now we can call the function by using its name.

```
hello()
```

PARAMETERS

If we want to make our functions more dynamic, we can define parameters. These parameters can then be processed in the function code.

```
def print_sum(number1, number2):
    print(number1 + number2)
```

As you can see, we have two parameters in between the parentheses – *number1* and *number2*. The function *print_sum* now prints the sum of these two values.

```
print_sum(20, 30)
```

This function call prints the value *50* out onto the screen.

RETURN VALUES

The two functions we wrote were just executing statements. What we can also do is return a certain value. This value can then be saved in a variable or it can be processed. For this, use the keyword *return*.

```
def add(number1, number2):
    return number1 + number2
```

Here we return the sum of the two parameters instead of printing it. But we can then use this result in our code.

```
number3 = add(10, 20)
print(add(10, 20))
```

DEFAULT PARAMETERS

Sometimes we want our parameters to have default values in case we don't specify anything else. We can do that by assigning values in the function definition.

```python
def say(text="Default Text"):
    print(text)
```

In this case, our function *say* prints the text that we pass as a parameter. But if we don't pass anything, it prints the default text.

VARIABLE PARAMETERS

Sometimes we want our functions to have a variable amount of parameters. For that, we use the *asterisk symbol* (*) in our parameters. We then treat the parameter as a sequence.

```python
def print_sum(*numbers):
    result = 0
    for x in numbers:
        result += x
    print(result)
```

Here we pass the parameter *numbers*. That may be five, ten or a hundred numbers. We then iterate over this parameter, add every value to our sum and print it.

```python
print_sum(10, 20, 30, 40)
```

SCOPES

The last thing we are going to talk about in this chapter is *scopes*. Scopes are not only important for functions but also for loops, conditions and other structures. Basically, we need to realize the difference between local and global variables.

```python
def function():
    number = 10
    print(number)

print(number) # Doesn't work
```

In this example, you see why it's important. When you define a variable inside of a function, a loop, a condition or anything similar, this variable can't be accessed outside of that structure. It doesn't exist.

```python
number = 10

def function():
    print(number)
```

This on the other hand works. The variable *number* was defined outside of the function, so it can be *seen* inside the function. But you will notice that you can't manipulate it.

In order to manipulate an object that was defined outside of the function, we need to define it as *global*.

```python
number = 10

def function():
```

```
global number
number += 10
print(number)
```

By using the keyword *global* we can fully access and manipulate the variable.

10 – Exception Handling

Programming is full of errors and exceptions. If you coded along while reading and experimented around a little bit, you may have encountered one or two error messages. These errors can also be called *exceptions*. They terminate our script and crash the program if they are not handled properly.

```
result = 10 / 0

Traceback (most recent call last):
  File "<pyshell#0>", line 1, in <module>
    10 / 0
ZeroDivisionError: division by zero
```

Just try to divide a number by zero and you will get a *ZeroDivisionError*. That's because a division by zero is not defined and our script doesn't know how to handle it. So it crashes.

```
text = "Hello"
number = int(text)

Traceback (most recent call last):
  File "<pyshell#2>", line 1, in <module>
    number = int(text)
ValueError: invalid literal for int() with base 10: 'Hello'
```

Alternatively, try to typecast an ordinary text into a number. You will get a *ValueError* and the script crashes again.

TRY EXCEPT

We can handle these errors or exceptions by defining *try* and *except* blocks.

```
try:
    print(10 / 0)
    text = "Hello"
    number = int(text)
except ValueError:
    print("Code for ValueError...")
except ZeroDivisionError:
    print("Code vor ZDE...")
except:
    print("Code for other exceptions...")
```

In the *try* block we put the code that we want to execute and where errors might occur. Then we define *except* blocks that tell our script what to do in case of the respective errors. Instead of crashing, we provide code that handles the situation. This might be a simple error message or a complex algorithm.

Here we defined two specific *except* blocks for the *ValueError* and the *ZeroDivisionError*. But we also defined a general *except* block in case we get an error that doesn't fit these two types.

ELSE STATEMENTS

We can also use else statements for code that gets executed if nothing went wrong.

```
try:
    print(10 / 0)
except:
    print("Error!")
else:
    print("Everything OK!")
```

FINALLY STATEMENTS

If we have some code that shall be executed at the end no matter what happened, we can write it into a *finally* block. This code will always be executed, even if an exception remains unhandled.

```
try:
    print(10 / 0)
except:
    print("Error!")
finally:
    print("Always executed!")
```

11 – FILE OPERATIONS

Oftentimes, we will need to read data in from external files or to save data into files. In this chapter we will take a look at *file streams* and the various operations.

OPENING AND CLOSING FILES

Before we can read from or write into a file, we first need to open a *file stream*. This returns the respective file as an object and allows us to deal with it.

```
file = open("myfile.txt", "r")
```

We use the function *open* in order to open a new file stream. As a parameter we need to define the file name and the *access mode* (we will talk about that in a second). The function returns the stream and we can save it into our variable *file*.

ACCESS MODES

Whenever we open a file in Python, we use a certain access mode. An access mode is the way in which we access a file. For example *reading* or *writing*. The following table gives you a quick overview over the various access modes.

ACCESS MODE

LETTER	ACCESS MODE
r	Reading
r+	Reading and Writing (No Truncating File)
rb	Reading Binary File
rb+	Reading and Writing Binary File (No Truncating File)
w	Writing
w+	Reading and Writing (Truncating File)
wb	Writing Binary File
wb+	Reading and Writing Binary File (Truncating File)
a	Appending
a+	Reading and Appending
ab	Appending Binary File
ab+	Reading and Appending Binary File

The difference between r+ or rb+ and w+ or wb+ is that w+ and wb+ overwrite existing files and create new ones if they don't exist. This is not the case for r+ and rb+.

CLOSING FILES

When we are no longer in need of our opened file stream, we should always close it. Python does this automatically in some cases but it is considered good practice to close streams manually. We close a stream by using the method *close*.

```
file = open("myfile.txt", "r+")
# CODE
file.close()
```

WITH STATEMENT

Alternatively, we can open and close streams more effectively by using *with* statements. A *with* statement opens a stream, executes the indented code and closes the stream afterwards.

```
with open("myfile.txt", "r") as file:
    # Some Code
```

It shortens the code and makes it easier to not forget to close your streams.

READING FROM FILES

Once we have opened a file in a reading mode, we can start reading its content. For this, we use the *read* method.

```
file = open('myfile.txt', 'r')
print(file.read())
file.close()
```

Here we open the file in reading mode and then print out its content. We can do the same thing by using the *with* statement.

```
with open('myfile.txt', 'r') as file:
    print(file.read())
```

But we don't have to read the whole file, if we don't want to. We can also read the first 20 or 50 characters by passing a parameter to the method.

```
with open('myfile.txt', 'r') as file:
    print(file.read(50))
```

WRITING INTO FILES

When we write into a file, we need to ask ourselves if we just want to add our text or if we want to completely overwrite a file. So we need to choose between writing and appending mode. For writing in general we use the method *write*.

```
file = open('myfile.txt', 'w')
print(file.write("Hello File!"))
file.flush()
file.close()
```

We open our file in writing mode and write our little text into the file. Notice that the text doesn't get written until we *flush* the stream. In this case this is not necessary because when we close a stream it flushes automatically. Let's look at the *with* statement alternative again.

```
with open('myfile.txt', 'w') as file:
    print(file.write("Hello File!"))
```

If we want to append our text, we just have to change the access mode. Everything else stays the same.

```
with open('myfile.txt', 'a') as file:
    print(file.write("Hello File!"))
```

OTHER OPERATIONS

Now if we want to perform other operations than writing, reading and appending, we will need to import and extra module. The basic Python functions and classes are available by default. But many things like mathematics, networking, threading and also additional file operations, require the import of modules. In this case we need to import the *os* module, which stands for operating system.

```python
import os
```

This would be one way to import this module. But if we do it like that, we would always need to specify the module when we use a function. To make it easier for us, we will do it like that.

```python
from os import *
```

Basically, what we are saying here is: Import all the function and classes from the module *os*. Notice that the import statements of a script should always be the first thing at the top.

DELETING AND RENAMING

For deleting and renaming files we have two very simple functions from the *os* module – *remove* and *rename*.

```python
remove("myfile.txt")
rename("myfile.txt", "newfile.txt")
```

We can also use the *rename* function, to move files into different directories. But the directory has to already be there. This function can't create new directories.

```
rename("myfile.txt", "newdir/myfile.txt")
```

DIRECTORY OPERATIONS

With the *os* module we can also operate with directories. We can create, delete and navigate through them.

```
mkdir("newdir")
chdir("newdir")
chdir("..")
rmdir("newdir")
```

Here we create a new directory by using the *mkdir* (make directory) function. We then go into that directory with the *chdir (change directory)* function and then back to the previous directory with the same function. Last but not least we remove the directory with the *rmdir (remove directory)* function.

By using *("..")* we navigate back one directory. Additionally, if we would want to specify a whole path like "C:\Users\Python\Desktop\file.txt", we would have to use double backslashes since Python uses single backslashes for different purposes. But we will talk about this in the next chapter in more detail.

12 – STRING FUNCTIONS

Even though strings are just texts or sequences of characters, we can apply a lot of functions and operations on them. Since this is a book for beginners, we won't get too much into the details here, but it is important for you to know how to deal with strings properly.

STRINGS AS SEQUENCES

As I already said, strings are sequences of characters and they can also be treated like that. We can basically index and slice the individual characters.

```
text = "Hello World!"
print(text[:5])
print(text[6:11])
```

The first slice we print is *"Hello"* and the second one is *"World"*. Another thing we can do is to iterate over strings with for loops.

```
text = "Hello World!"
for x in text:
    print(x)
```

In this example, we print the individual characters one after the other.

ESCAPE CHARACTERS

In strings we can use a lot of different *escape characters*. These are non-printable characters like *tab* or *new line*. They are all initiated by a backslash, which is the reason why we need to use double backslashes for file paths (see last chapter).

The following table summarizes the most important of these escape characters. If you are interested in all the other ones just use google but you won't need them for now.

ESCAPE CHARATCERS	
NOTATION	**DESCRIPTION**
\b	Backspace
\n	New Line
\s	Space
\t	Tab

STRING FORMATTING

When we have a text which shall include the values of variables, we can use the % operator and placeholders, in order to insert our values.

```
name, age = "John", 25
print("%s is my name!" % name)
print("I am %d years old!" % age)
```

Notice that we used different placeholders for different data types. We use *%s* for strings and *%d* for integers. The following table shows you which placeholders are needed for which data types.

PLACEHOLDERS	
PLACEHOLDER	**DATA TYPE**
%c	Character
%s	String
%d or %i	Integer
%f	Float
%e	Exponential Notation

If you want to do it more general without specifying data types, you can use the *format* function.

```
name, age = "John", 25
print("My name is {} and I am {} years old"
      .format(name, age))
```

Here we use curly brackets as placeholders and insert the values afterwards using the *format* function.

STRING FUNCTIONS

There are a ton of string functions in Python and it would be unnecessary and time wasting to talk about all of them in this book. If you want an overview just go online and look for them. One website, where you can find them is W3Schools.

W3Schools Python String Functions:
https://www.w3schools.com/python/python_ref_string.asp

In this chapter however, we will focus on the most essential, most interesting and most important of these functions. The ones that you might need in the near future.

CASE MANIPULATING FUNCTIONS

We have five different case manipulating string functions in Python. Let's have a look at them.

CASE MANIPULATING FUNCTIONS	
FUNCTION	**DESCRIPTION**
string.lower()	Converts all letters to lowercase
string.upper()	Converts all letters to uppercase
string.title()	Converts all letters to titlecase
string.capitalize()	Converts first letter to uppercase
string.swapcase()	Swaps the case of all letters

COUNT FUNCTION

If you want to count how many times a specific string occurs in another string, you can use the *count* function.

```
text = "I like you and you like me!"
print(text.count("you"))
```

In this case, the number two will get printed, since the string *"you"* occurs two times.

FIND FUNCTION

In order to find the first occurrence of a certain string in another string, we use the *find* function.

```
text = "I like you and you like me!"
print(text.find("you"))
```

Here the result is 7 because the first occurrence of *"you"* is at the index 7.

JOIN FUNCTION

With the *join* function we can join a sequence to a string and separate each element by this particular string.

```
names = ["Mike", "John", "Anna"]
sep = "-"
print(sep.join(names))
```

The result looks like this: Mike-John-Anna

REPLACE FUNCTION

The *replace* function replaces one string within a text by another one. In the following example, we replace the name *John* by the name *Anna*.

```
text = "I like John and John is my friend!"
text = text.replace("John", "Anna")
```

SPLIT FUNCTION

If we want to split specific parts of a string and put them into a list, we use the *split* function.

```
names = "John,Max,Bob,Anna"
name_list = names.split(",")
```

Here we have a string of names separated by commas. We then use the *split* function and define the comma as the separator in order to save the individual names into a list.

TRIPLE QUOTES

The last topic of this chapter is *triple quotes*. They are just a way to write multi-line strings without the need of escape characters.

```
print('''Hello World!
This is a multi-line comment!

And we don't need to use escape characters
in order to write new empty lines!''')
```

What's Next?

You made it! We covered all of the core basics of Pythons. You now understand how this language is structured but also general programming principles like conditions, loops and functions. Definitely, you are now able to develop a basic calculator or other simple applications. But the journey has just begun.

This is only the first part of the Python Bible Series. We've covered the topics for beginners but the real fun starts when we get into more advanced topics like network programming, threading, machine learning, data science, finance, neural networks and more. With this book you have an excellent basis for the next volumes of the Python Bible and I encourage you to continue your journey.

The next part will be for intermediates and advanced programmers, which you know belong to. So stay tuned and keep coding!

Last but not least, a little reminder. This book was written for you, so that you can get as much value as possible and learn to code effectively. If you find this book valuable or you think you learned something new, please write a quick review on Amazon. It is completely free and takes about one minute. But it helps me produce more high quality books, which you can benefit from.

Thank you!

NeuralNine

If you are interested in free educational content about programming and machine learning, check out https://www.neuralnine.com/

There we have free blog posts, videos and more for you! Also, you can follow the ***@neuralnine*** Instagram account for daily infographics about programming and AI!

Website: https://www.neuralnine.com/

Instagram: @neuralnine

YouTube: NeuralNine

www.ingramcontent.com/pod-product-compliance
Lightning Source LLC
Chambersburg PA
CBHW051214050326
40689CB00008B/1301